STEAM JOBS
FOR
GEARHEADS

BY SAM RHODES

CAPSTONE PRESS
a capstone imprint

Edge Books are published by Capstone Press,
1710 Roe Crest Drive
North Mankato, Minnesota 56003
www.mycapstone.com

Library of Congress Cataloging-in-Publication Data
Names: Rhodes, Sam (Samuel David) 1983- author.
Title: STEAM jobs for gearheads / by Sam Rhodes.
Description: North Mankato, Minnesota : Capstone Press, [2019] |
    Series: Edge books. STEAM jobs. | Audience: Ages 8-14.
Identifiers: LCCN 2018006064 (print) | LCCN 2018012224 (ebook) |
    ISBN 9781543531022 (eBook PDF) | ISBN 9781543530940 (hardcover) |
    ISBN 9781543530988 (pbk.)
Subjects: LCSH: Engineering—Vocational guidance—Juvenile literature. |
    Machinists—Vocational guidance—Juvenile literature. |
    LCGFT: Instructional and educational works.
Classification: LCC TA157 (ebook) | LCC TA157 .R485 2019 (print) | DDC 629.28/7023—dc23
LC record available at https://lccn.loc.gov/2018006064

Editorial Credits
Editor: Lauren Dupuis-Perez
Book Designer: Sara Radka
Production Specialist: Kathy McColley

Image Credits
Getty Images: Anton_Sokolov, 7 (top), Brendon Thorne, 9, Caiaimage/Agnieszka Olek, 17, 22,
Caiaimage/Chris Ryan, 25, Christopher Jue, 24, Cultura/Monty Rakusen, 20, 21 (bottom), EyeEm/
Khanti Jantasao, 15 (top), Handout, cover (back), 21 (top), Hero Images, 12, 23 (bottom), 28,
29 (bottom), Jetta Productions, cover (foreground), Joe Raedle, 16, monkeybusinessimages, 11,
monstArrr_, 23 (top), Philartphace, 14, PhonlamaiPhoto, 29 (top), Stewart Sutton, 26, Stockbyte, 4,
Zero Creatives, 27 (bottom); NASA: 19; Newscom: Castelli/AND/Sipa USA, 10, Workhorse Group/
Cover Images, 18, ZUMA Press/Daily News/Evan Yee, 15 (bottom); Pixabay: PellissierJP, cover
(background), 1; Shutterstock: Alvov, 27 (top), betto rodrigues, 8, cristovao, 7 (bottom), Denis Z.,
13 (top), Marafona, 6, Nejron Photo, 13 (bottom)

Printed and bound in the USA.
PA017

TABLE OF CONTENTS

INTRODUCTION
FULL STEAM AHEAD

Custom motorcycle builders use their artistic skills and knowledge of mechanics to create one-of-a-kind bikes.

Gearheads love machines, especially cars and other vehicles. It's not just what these machines can do that gearheads enjoy. It's how they do it. Gearheads are curious. They love taking things apart, inspecting how they work, and putting them back together. A car breaks down. Gearheads want to know why. A motorcycle isn't fast enough. Gearheads want to **modify** the engine to make it more powerful. Understanding and fixing machines is what drives gearheads.

Many jobs that appeal to gearheads are STEAM-related. STEAM stands for science, technology, engineering, art, and math. An education that is STEAM-focused can lead to many rewarding careers, and many of these jobs are perfect for gearheads.

Almost every industry today depends on machines. These machines need to be designed, built, repaired, and modified. Gearheads use their skills to keep these machines running. From working on custom motorcycles to massive cargo ships, gearheads have many ways to take their careers full steam ahead!

modify—to change in some way

CHAPTER 1
CLASSIC CAR BUILDERS

NEW LEASE ON LIFE

An old car with a worn out engine and missing parts may seem useless to some. But others look at it and see potential. They see a car that was beautiful once and could be again. All it needs is some time and attention.

It can be rewarding to turn rusty old vehicles into gleaming works of art. Restoration can be a minor or a major job. It all depends on the age and condition of the car. Each part of car restoration requires special skills. It can include mechanical work, painting, **fabrication**, electrical wiring, and interior restoration.

A classic car can be rebuilt from just the body. This type of project can take hundreds of hours of work.

Car restoration offers many unique challenges. A part might need to be replaced that is not available to buy. When this happens, restorers may have to create the part themselves. Some restorers design the needed part on a computer and then print it using a 3-D printer. Many older cars have wiring that needs to be completely replaced. Some clients even want restorers to add new technology to old cars, such as advanced stereo systems, special brakes, and seat warmers.

Restorers must focus on details when working on the interior **upholstery**. Not just any material will do. Many restorers use the same fabrics for seats and flooring that the vehicle had originally. This makes the restored car as close to the original as possible.

EDUCATION

Classic car builders should have a strong background in the following STEAM subjects:

- **visual art**
- **electrical engineering**
- **mechanical engineering**

fabrication—the building and shaping of the parts of a car

upholstery—materials used to make a soft covering, such as for seats

A hot rod builder creates an original pattern and blends carefully selected colors for a custom flame paint job.

HOT RODS

Many gearheads take old cars and update them to be quicker and slicker. Generally hot rods are any cars that have been updated from their original production models to be more powerful and faster. Hot rod builders increase engine power and remove unnecessary parts to make the cars go faster.

STEAM FACT

Wally Parks created the National Hot Rod Association (NHRA) in 1951 to organize car races and events.

Hot rod builders must be excellent engineers. They may need to fix up a damaged frame, cleaning it and replacing any damaged parts. They might also build a new frame entirely by welding steel tubing together.

Hot rod builders often need to fix up an old engine. They might replace parts, fix other parts, and add new parts to increase the engine's power.

People want to show off their hot rods, so hot rod builders must have an artistic eye. Some hot rod owners display their cars in shows. Other owners just want to cruise their hot rods around on the streets. A unique paint job is important either way. Bold colors can make a car stand out from the crowd. Bright flames are a classic hot rod look.

CARS ON TV

Over the years cars have proven to be a big draw for TV audiences. Shows such as *Fast N' Loud* and *Counting Cars* focus on restoration and modification. Other shows, such as *Top Gear*, test and review different cars, often pushing them to their limits. In 2013 *Top Gear* claimed the Guinness World Record for the most-watched factual TV show.

Top Gear

CHAPTER 2
MARINE ARCHITECTS

With ocean breezes, the smell of salt air, and endless entertainment, cruises make for great family vacations. But who designs the ships that make this possible? Marine architects lead the design of big ships. They design cargo ships, cruise ships, yachts, and even submarines.

Marine architects must carefully consider appearance and performance. Large ships today are typically made of steel. Steel does not float. Marine architects use math principles called **buoyancy** and **displacement** to keep heavy ships from sinking. Architects use the same principles to ensure that ships remain stable during storms.

One of the world's largest cruise ships is called *Harmony of the Seas*. It can hold almost 9,000 people.

STEAM FACT

Marine architects also design remotely operated vehicles (ROVs) for deep-sea research.

Computers are the primary tool in the design process. The marine architect uses computer modeling software to design every aspect of the ship. **Geometry** is important when designing the ship's **hull**. A marine architect might choose a longer, thinner hull to create a faster ship. A wider hull might be used if the ship will have to carry a lot of cargo.

Other parts of ship design are safety and energy efficiency. Marine architects research and develop materials and designs that reduce fuel costs. Marine architects design oil tankers with double hulls. This prevents an oil spill even if the outer hull is damaged.

EDUCATION

Marine architects should have a strong background in the following STEAM subjects:

- calculus
- physics
- mechanical engineering

buoyancy—the tendency of an object to float or rise when in water

displacement—the weight of the water a ship pushes away

geometry—a field of math that studies the relationships between lines, shapes, and three-dimensional figures

hull—the frame or body of a ship or aircraft

CHAPTER 3
CUSTOM MOTORCYCLE BUILDERS

Dozens of motorcycles sit outside the world-famous Rock Store outside of Los Angeles, California. One biker revs her engine. She holds the front brake and twists the throttle. The engine roars to life as the back tire spins. Smoke and the smell of rubber surround the biker.

Showing off a bike is a big part of motorcycle culture. Instead of buying from a dealership, many bikers choose to have a motorcycle built specifically for them. Custom building a motorcycle usually requires hiring a specialist.

Demand for custom motorcycles is growing around the world.

STEAM FACT

In 2015 Bharat Sinh Parmar built the longest motorcycle in the world. It is 86.3 feet (26.3 meters) long.

Some custom motorcycles have V-twin engines. The two engine cylinders form a V shape.

The first step is designing the bike. Builders use computer software to design the bike according to their customer's needs. When building for a specific person, the motorcycle can be fitted to the rider exactly. Custom builders use geometry to determine the angles and distances of the handlebars, seat, and frame. This makes the motorcycle comfortable and safe.

Once the design is complete, the motorcycle builder begins to make the parts. Most of the bike will be made of metal. Builders use hand tools to cut, shape, weld, and drill metal parts. The builders use computer-controlled cutting tools to make more detailed parts, such as wheels. With all the parts made, the bike is painted and assembled. The motorcycle is finally ready to cruise the streets.

EDUCATION

Custom motorcycle builders should have a strong background in the following STEAM subjects:

- **mechanical engineering**
- **geometry**
- **calculus**

CHAPTER 4

ROLLER COASTER DESIGNERS

The cars click up a massive hill. They come to a near-complete stop at the top. Suddenly, the coaster begins to slide forward, slowly at first and then impossibly fast. Enjoying the thrilling ride, the riders are not thinking about all the careful planning that went into it. That is the job of the roller coaster designer.

The coaster designer uses both technology and materials science to create the best ride possible. The designer uses computer software to explore different ideas and themes. The designer decides what materials should be used to make the track. Wooden roller coasters sway, making for a wilder ride. Steel roller coasters have a smoother, faster ride.

Most loops are on steel roller coasters.

Building a roller coaster always starts with understanding **physics.** Have you ever wondered why the first hill of a roller coaster is always the biggest? The first big hill provides the **potential energy** to carry the cars through the rest of the ride. **Friction** causes the cars to lose energy as they travel. The designer carefully plans all the hills, loops, and corkscrews, making sure the cars have enough energy to reach the end of the track.

Most importantly, the ride must be safe. A coaster designer must have knowledge of structural engineering. They use this knowledge to make sure that the coaster is strong and supported. After the coaster is designed and approved, the designer passes the project on to a team to build it.

EDUCATION

Roller coaster designers should have a strong background in the following STEAM subjects:

- **materials science**
- **physics**
- **engineering**
- **calculus**

physics—the study of matter and energy, including light, heat, electricity, and motion

potential energy—the stored energy of an object that is raised, stretched, or squeezed

friction—a force created when two objects rub together; friction slows down objects

CHAPTER 5
AEROSPACE ENGINEERS

TAKING FLIGHT

A brand-new jet screams across the cloudless blue sky. After enduring pretend lightning strikes, extreme pressure trials, and wear-and-tear tests, the final round of preparation has begun. A test pilot takes this new jet out for a spin. The pilot will encounter **crosswinds**, extreme altitudes that affect flight performance, and ice buildup. The aerospace engineers want to see how it holds up.

From **aerodynamics** to structural concerns, aerospace engineers consider many details when designing aircraft. For example, engineers might adjust the wings to make a plane more stable or fast. The environmental impact of airplanes is a big concern for airlines. Aerospace engineers are constantly working to design more efficient engines and more aerodynamic planes.

STEAM FACT

Leonardo da Vinci was the first to design and sketch a flying machine. It was called an ornithopter. It had wings that flapped like a bird.

Designing aircraft for outer space comes with unique challenges. Spaceships must move into and out of Earth's atmosphere. This creates a large amount of stress on the spaceship. Aerospace engineers are required to have structural engineering skills to make a ship that can withstand these forces. Many space vehicles are unmanned. They can complete many tasks on their own, but still require some manual remote control. Aerospace engineers design these remote control systems.

Aerospace engineers test their designs in a controlled setting and out in the field. Wind tunnels test an aircraft's aerodynamics. Test pilots fly new planes while engineers monitor the systems from the ground.

EDUCATION

Aerospace engineers should have a strong background in the following STEAM subjects:

- **calculus**
- **physics**
- **computer science**

crosswind—a wind that blows across the path of an airplane, ship, or other moving object

aerodynamics—the ability of something to move easily and quickly through the air

FLYING INTO THE FUTURE

Today aerospace engineers might create new drones, flying cars, and even jetpacks. These new technologies have opened up an exciting world of aerospace engineering. Militaries, police departments, and fire departments use drones. They are also rapidly becoming an important tool for agriculture and some other businesses. Some drones need to be fast. Other drones might need to carry heavy boxes or fly long distances. Aerospace engineers work to meet each need.

Some experts believe drones that carry people will be operating in cities around the world by 2022.

MARS ROVER CURIOSITY

The 2012 landing of the Mars rover *Curiosity* was a big accomplishment for aerospace engineers. They had successfully transported a science laboratory the size of a small car to a planet 140 million miles (225 million kilometers) away.

Engineers designed a complex remote control system for the rover. The rover fell to Mars at 13,200 miles (21,243 km) per hour. Engineers built rockets that fired automatically to keep the rover on course. An ultra-strong parachute slowed down the rover as it neared the surface. NASA called the project the most elaborate and challenging mission in the history of robotic space flight.

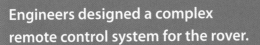

Jetpacks used to be machines of science fiction. They seemed impossible to build. After decades of experiments, aerospace engineers have finally succeeded. They've made engines small and powerful enough to carry a person. They also found a way to control the engines. Jetpack Aviation cofounder and aerospace engineer Nelson Tyler created a device with two engines. Each engine rotates separately. This helps keep the jetpack stable and controlled.

CHAPTER 6
RACE ENGINEERS

One small change to the engine can improve a race car's speed and help it win more races.

In car racing every second counts. It is no wonder this profession attracts gearheads who love to go fast. Race engineers work with the rest of the racing team to design the best race car possible.

STEAM FACT

The most experienced race engineers can make $150,000 per year.

McLaren MCL33
Formula One car

Engineers create race cars with special attention to speed, safety, and cost. They usually use a computer for the initial design work. Race engineers run computer **simulations** to try out different body designs. They might use physics to create effective **spoilers**.

Some race engineers also work on race days. They might help set up the car. They consider weather conditions and track conditions. During the race the engineers might monitor data on a computer. They tell the driver if there are any problems. After the race the engineers may run performance tests. The engineers collect and study data so that the car improves after each race.

EDUCATION
Race team engineers should have a strong background in the following STEAM subjects:

- **algebra**
- **physics**
- **mechanical engineering**

simulation—a computer model of something in real life

spoiler—a wing-shaped part attached to a car that helps improve the car's handling

CHAPTER 7
MACHINISTS

A drill bit spins. Small, shiny flakes fly into the air. Like a knife slicing through warm butter, the spinning bit carves into a solid piece of metal. Little by little, the metal block turns into a detailed piece of machinery.

There are about 500,000 machinists working in the United States.

Machinists design and make metal parts for automobiles, airplanes, and industrial machines from raw metal. Before they begin, they work closely with engineers to decide on the best methods, materials, shapes, and sizes for the project.

Once the part is designed, the machinist makes it. Machinists use enormous computer numerical controlled (CNC) machines to cut and shape metal. Precision is everything. Machinists must craft the parts to the exact measurements specified.

EDUCATION

Machinists should have a strong background in the following STEAM subjects:

- **geometry**
- **metalworking**
- **materials science**

Finally, machinists must test parts for quality control. Machinists must make sure the finished parts are strong enough. They use their knowledge of metals to figure out the part's **tolerance**. Then the machinist must inspect the part to ensure it fits in the machine and is free of defects.

tolerance—how much a part's measurements, such as length, weight, and thickness, can differ from the plans to create it

CHAPTER 8
AUTOMOTIVE JOURNALISTS

WRITE ON!

Gearheads who love cars but don't love getting dirty can become automotive journalists. Automotive journalists share information from makers of cars and trucks with the public. It's a tricky job. Automotive journalists need to understand technical concepts. They also need a creative, artistic mind to communicate these ideas clearly.

The Tokyo Motor Show is Japan's biggest car show. It draws about 800,000 visitors.

Many journalists work for companies that produce magazines, newspapers, and website content. They have editors who assign them stories. They also suggest stories to their editors. The automotive journalist usually takes pictures or videos to go with a story. After the article is written, an editor will review it and suggest edits.

Automotive journalists often review new cars on the market. Journalists will research the vehicle and the car company. They may interview representatives from the company. They will test-drive the new car to see how it handles, what features it has, and how comfortable it is on the road. Once automotive journalists have written their review of the new car, they work with editors to improve and prepare the article to be published.

STEAM FACT

Automotive journalist Jason Harper estimated that he drove almost $10 million worth of cars in less than six months on the job.

EDUCATION

Automotive journalists should have a strong background in the following STEAM subjects:

- **creative writing**
- **photography and videography**
- **desktop publishing**

CHAPTER 9
SHIP ENGINEERS

A storm is coming. People race around the swaying ship's deck, trying to prepare. On the high seas, a large storm can be dangerous. It can also damage machinery. In the engine room, the ship engineer quickly closes all the watertight doors. He ties down loose equipment and checks the engine. Speaking to the captain over a radio, the engineer suggests adjustments to safely travel through the storm.

Ship engineers work for cruise lines, shipping companies, and militaries. They maintain the engines of ships while they are at sea. The stakes are high in this job. Ship engineers keep expensive ships operational. The safety of the people and cargo onboard is their responsibility. They work on tanker ships, cargo ships, cruise liners, oil drilling platforms, and other types of ships.

STEAM FACT
Ships carry about 90 percent of all goods traded in the world.

Ship engineers working in the oil and gas industry maintain the engines of oil tankers.

Ship engineers repair and maintain everything mechanical, electrical, and structural on the ship. This is a huge task. The engineers routinely take apart machines that are broken. They examine the various parts to find out what is wrong. They must then repair any broken or worn parts and reassemble the machine.

Ship engineers also keep watch on all the mechanical systems to prevent problems. They read gauges and take measurements. They keep detailed logs of equipment performance. Another ongoing responsibility of ship engineers is ordering replacement parts and maintenance supplies.

EDUCATION

Ship engineers should have a strong background in the following STEAM subjects:

- **calculus**
- **physics**
- **mechanical engineering**

CHAPTER 10
ROBOTICS ENGINEERS

A car moves quickly down an assembly line. All around, parts are pieced together, welded, and adjusted. It is not people doing this work, though. Robots build these cars. But who builds the robots? This is the job of a robotics engineer.

Robotics engineers design and build many types of robots. They engineer factory robots, toy robots, medical robots, and more. Robotics engineering combines mechanical engineering, electrical engineering, and computer technology.

Robotics engineers monitor and maintain industrial robots.

Industrial robots work in factories and perform repetitive tasks. Engineers can program them to do jobs, such as stacking crates of food or welding car parts. They usually have no sensors. They will continue to move as programmed even if someone gets in their way. This can be dangerous. For this reason, robotics engineers must program safety precautions. Electronic fencing that activates a **kill switch** is one example. It can prevent injury if someone gets too close to an industrial robot.

Robotics engineers design both modern and futuristic robots. The global focus on **green energy** is creating a demand for robotics. Green-energy farms use robotics to collect and send energy. Robotics engineers are also creating robots with **artificial intelligence** (AI). This allows robots to learn new tasks. Today's AI robots can recognize and respond to speech, recognize faces, and do many other tasks.

EDUCATION

Robotics engineers should have a strong background in the following STEAM subjects:

- **physics**
- **electrical engineering**
- **mechanical engineering**

kill switch—a device that shuts off a machine's engine

green energy—power obtained from natural sources, such as wind, water, and sunlight, that is used to create electricity

artificial intelligence—the ability of a machine to think like a person

GLOSSARY

aerodynamics (air-oh-dy-NA-miks)—the ability of something to move easily and quickly through the air

artificial intelligence (ar-ti-FISH-uhl in-TEL-uh-junss)—the ability of a machine to think like a person

buoyancy (BOI-yuhn-see)—the tendency of an object to float or rise when in water

crosswind (KROS-wind)—a wind that blows across the path of an airplane, ship, or other moving object

displacement (dis-PLAYS-muhnt)—the weight of the water a ship pushes away

fabrication (fab-ri-KAY-shuhn)—the building and shaping of the parts of a car

friction (FRIK-shuhn)—a force created when two objects rub together; friction slows down objects

geometry (jee-OM-uh-tree)—a field of math that studies the relationships between lines, shapes, and three-dimensional figures

green energy (GREEN EN-ur-jee)—power obtained from natural sources, such as wind, water, and sunlight, that is used to create electricity

hull (HUL)—the frame or body of a ship or aircraft

kill switch (KIL SWICH)—a device that shuts off a machine's engine

modify (MOD-ih-fye)—to change in some way

physics (FIZ-iks)—the study of matter and energy, including light, heat, electricity, and motion

potential energy (puh-TEN-shuhl EN-ur-jee)—the stored energy of an object that is raised, stretched, or squeezed

simulation (sim-yuh-LAY-shuhn)—a computer model of something in real life

spoiler (SPOIL-uhr)—a wing-shaped part attached to a car that helps improve the car's handling

tolerance (TOL-ur-uhnce)—how much a part's measurements, such as length, weight, and thickness, can differ from the plans to create it

upholstery (uhp-HOHL-stuh-ree)—a soft covering, such as for seats

READ MORE

Bolte, Mari. *The Amazing Story of the Combustion Engine.* Max Axiom STEM Adventures. North Mankato, Minn.: Capstone, 2014.

Conklin, Wendy. *Enhancing Engineering.* STEM Careers. Huntington Beach, Calif.: Teacher Created Materials, 2017.

Katirgis, Jane. *STEM Jobs with Cars.* STEM Jobs You'll Love. Vero Beach, Fla.: Rourke Educational Media, 2015.

INTERNET SITES

Use FactHound to find Internet sites related to this book.

Visit *www.facthound.com*

Just type in 9781543530940 and go.

Check out projects, games and lots more at
www.capstonekids.com

INDEX